Contents

Foreword 2	Green Plants: Growth And Nutrition 1 26
How To Use This Book 3	Green Plants: Growth And Nutrition 2 28
Life Processes: Humans And Animals 4	The Parts Of A Flower 30
Life Processes: Plants 6	Pollination And Fertilisation 32
Teeth 8	Seeds And Fruits 34
Nutrition 10	Living Things In Their Environments ..36
Circulation: The Heart 12	Food Chains 38
Circulation: Exercise 14	Micro-Organisms 40
Movement 16	Classifying Animals And Plants 42
Growth And Reproduction 18	Keys 44
Healthy Lives 1 20	Answers 46
Healthy Lives 2 22	
The Structure Of Green Plants 24	**Check Your Progress!** 48

AUTHOR: Camilla de la Bédoyère
EDITORIAL: John Cattermole, Vicky Garrard, Julia Rolf
DESIGN: Jen Bishop, Dave Jones
ILLUSTRATORS: Bridget Dowty, Sarah Wimperis
PRODUCTION: Chris Herbert, Claire Walker

COMMISSIONING EDITOR: Polly Willis
PUBLISHER AND CREATIVE DIRECTOR: Nick Wells

3 book Pack ISBN 1-84451-088-3   Book ISBN 1-84451-046-8
6 book Pack ISBN 1-84451-090-5   Book ISBN 1-84451-101-4

First published in 2004

A copy of the CIP data for this book is available from the British Library upon request.

All rights reserved. No part of this publication may be reproduced, stored in a retrieval system, or transmitted in any form or by any means, without the prior written permission of the copyright holder.

Created and produced by
FLAME TREE PUBLISHING
Crabtree Hall,
Crabtree Lane,
Fulham, London SW6 6TY
United Kingdom
www.flametreepublishing.com

Flame Tree Publishing is part of The Foundry Creative Media Co. Ltd.

© The Foundry Creative Media Co. Ltd, 2004

Printed in Croatia

Foreword

Sometimes when I am crossing the playground on my way to visit a primary school I pass young children playing at schools. There is always a stern authoritarian little teacher at the front laying down the law to the unruly group of children in the pretend class. This puzzles me a little because the school I am visiting is very far from being like the children's play. Where do they get this Victorian view of what school is like? Perhaps it's handed down from generation to generation through the genes. Certainly they don't get it from their primary school. Teachers today are more often found alongside their pupils, who are learning by actually doing things for themselves, rather than merely listening and obeying instructions.

Busy children, interested and involved in their classroom reflect what we know about how they learn. Of course they learn from teachers but most of all they learn from their experience of life and their life is spent both in and out of school. Indeed, if we compare the impact upon children of even the finest schools and teachers, we find that three or four times as great an impact is made by the reality of children's lives outside the school. That reality has the parent at the all important centre. No adult can have so much impact, for good or ill, as the young child's mother or father.

This book, and others in the series, are founded on the sure belief that the great majority of parents want to help their children grow and learn and that teachers are keen to support them. The days when parents were kept at arm's length from schools are long gone and over the years we have moved well beyond the white line painted on the playground across which no parent must pass without an appointment. Now parents move freely in and out of schools and very often are found in the classrooms backing up the teachers. Both sides of the partnership know how important it is that children should be challenged and stimulated both in and out of school.

Perhaps the most vital part of this book is where parents and children are encouraged to develop activities beyond those offered on the page. The more the children explore and use the ideas and techniques we want them to learn, the more they will make new knowledge of their very own. It's not just getting the right answer, it's growing as a person through gaining skill in action and not only in books. The best way to learn is to live.

I remember reading a story to a group of nine year old boys. The story was about soldiers and of course the boys, bloodthirsty as ever, were hanging on my every word. I came to the word khaki and I asked the group "What colour is khaki?" One boy was quick to answer. "Silver" he said, "It's silver." "Silver? I queried. "Yes," he said with absolute confidence, "silver, my Dad's car key is silver." Now I reckon I'm a pretty good teller of stories to children but when it came down to it, all my dramatic reading of a gripping story gave way immediately to the power of the boy's experience of life. That meant so much more to him, as it does to all children.

JOHN COE
General Secretary, National Association for Primary Education (NAPE).

Parents and teachers work together in NAPE to improve the quality of learning and teaching in primary schools. We campaign hard for a better deal for children at the vital early stage of their education upon which later success depends. We are always pleased to hear from parents.

NAPE, Moulton College, Moulton, Northampton, NN3 7RR,
Telephone: 01604 647 646 Web: www.nape.org.uk

How To Use This Book

Living Things is one of six books in the **Revision, Practice & Home Learning** series, which has been devised to help you support your child as they revise for their SATs at the end of Year Six.

The National Curriculum gives teachers clear guidelines on what subjects should be studied in Science, and to what level. These guidelines have been used to form the content of both this book and **Materials & Physical Processes**, the second Science text in this series.

Each page contains revision notes, exercises for your child to complete, an activity they can complete away from the book (**Activity** boxes) and practical pointers to give you extra information and guidance (**Parents Start Here** boxes). At the end of the book you will find a checklist of topics, where you can mark off each topic as it is mastered.

This book has been designed for children to work through alone, but it is recommended that you read the book first to acquaint yourself with the material it contains. Try to be at hand when your child is working with the book; your input is valuable. The influence science exerts on our society is increasing at an ever greater rate. Sadly, many parents feel that science is something they know little about – this book may help you overcome gaps in your own knowledge and thus be in a better position to teach your child.

Encourage good study habits in your child:

- Try to set aside a short time every day for studying. Ten to 20 minutes a day is plenty.

- Establish a quiet and comfortable environment for your child to work and suitable tools, e.g. sharp pencils and good handwriting pens.

- Give your child access to drinking water whenever they work; research suggests this helps them to perform better.

- Reward your child; plenty of praise for good work motivates children to succeed.

- Ensure your child eats a healthy diet, gets plenty of rest and lots of opportunity to play.

This book is intended to support your child in their school work. Sometimes children find particular topics hard to understand; discuss this with their teacher, who may be able to suggest alternative ways to help your child.

KS2: Living Things

Parents Start Here...

The syllabus requires that children explore ideas in science and the way that scientific exploration is carried out. Researching the lives and work of great scientists is one way to do this.

Top Tip! Always look for positive aspects to your child's work as well as helping them to resolve errors.

Life Processes: Humans And Animals

Remember!

- There are seven life processes. They are: nutrition, movement, growth, respiration, excretion, sensitivity and reproduction.
- The way that animals and plants carry out their life processes is often linked to their environments.

Circle the correct answers to these questions:

1. The life process which describes how an animal breathes oxygen into its lungs is called:

a) excretion   b) **respiration**   c) growth   d) sensitivity

2. The life process which describes how an animal gets from one place to another is called:

a) excretion   b) growth   c) nutrition   d) **movement**

3. The life process which describes how a plant gets rid of the oxygen it no longer needs is called:

a) growth   b) reproduction   c) nutrition   d) excretion

4. The life process which describes how animals eat food is called:

a) reproduction   b) respiration   c) nutrition   d) sensitivity

Life Processes: Humans And Animals

5. The life process which describes how animals and plants produce offspring is called:

a) reproduction **b)** respiration **c)** excretion **d)** movement

6. The life process which describes how an animal or plant increases in size and changes with age is called:

a) movement **b)** (growth) **c)** nutrition **d)** reproduction

7. The life process which describes how an animal or plant responds to changes in the environment is called:

a) reproduction **b)** sensitivity **c)** nutrition **d)** movement

8. Write the names of the seven life processes:

_____   _____

_____   _____

_____   _____

_____

Activity

Edward Jenner coined the word 'vaccination', from the Latin word **vaccinia** which means 'cowpox'. Investigate the life-saving work of Edward Jenner and find out how his discovery has saved many thousands of lives.

Check Your Progress!
Life Processes: Humans And Animals
Turn to page 48 and put a tick next to what you have just learned.

KS2: Living Things

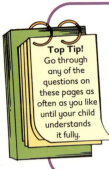

Top Tip! Go through any of the questions on these pages as often as you like until your child understands it fully.

Parents Start Here...

Communication of ideas and scientific processes is a key part of the curriculum. Encourage your child to use the appropriate vocabulary whenever you discuss science subjects together.

Life Processes: Plants

Remember!

- **Nutrition:** plants make their own food using sunlight, carbon dioxide and water.
- **Movement:** plant stems move towards the light.
- **Respiration:** plants breathe carbon dioxide in. They use this gas to make food.
- **Excretion:** oxygen is a waste product of plant respiration.
- Gases move in and out of plants through their leaves.
- **Sensitivity:** plants are sensitive to light and temperature.
- **Reproduction:** plants usually reproduce by seed.

Tick the correct answers to these questions:

1. Which of these shows that a plant can move?
   a) It grows a flower. ☐
   b) Its stem bends towards a window. ✓
   c) It waves about in the wind. ☐
   d) Seeds get carried by the wind. ☐

2. The gas that plants need to make food is:
   a) oxygen ✓
   b) air ☐
   c) carbon dioxide ☐
   d) nitrogen ☐

Life Processes: Plants

3. Plants need water to live because:
   a) they use it to make their own food ☐
   b) it keeps their roots moist ☑
   c) it keeps them green ☐
   d) they get thirsty ☐

4. A seed is:
   a) a food storage unit ☐
   b) a way that a plant can move from one place to another ☐
   c) the way that most plants reproduce ☑
   d) a method of excretion ☐

5. Some flowers close at night but are open in the day. This shows that:
   a) Plants are sensitive to the moon ☐
   b) Plants are sensitive to the light ☑
   c) Plants can not breathe during the night ☐
   d) Plants can not move when it is dark ☐

6. The gas that plants excrete is:
   a) carbon dioxide ☐
   b) oxygen ☑
   c) nitrogen ☐
   d) helium ☐

Activity

TRY THIS

You have probably heard people talk about the destruction of the tropical rainforests. Why do you think these places matter? Rainforests are sometimes called the 'lungs of the planet'. Why do you think they have this nickname?

Check Your Progress!
Life Processes: Plants ☐
Turn to page 48 and put a tick next to what you have just learned.

KS2: Living Things

Top Tip! Remember to give your child lots of praise – they will work so much better.

Parents Start Here...

Children are expected to think about how an animal's teeth are suitable for their diet which is, in turn, partly determined by the available food sources and environment. Help your child see how these factors are all linked.

Teeth

Remember!

- Teeth break up food into smaller pieces so it can be digested.
- Humans and animals have teeth that are best suited to the types of food they eat.
- Canine teeth are best for grinding and chewing food.
- Molars are best for cutting and chopping food, especially grass.
- Incisor teeth are best for tearing food, especially meat.
- Humans have two sets of teeth.
- We need to take care of our teeth.

1. Label the teeth:

   a) _____

   b) _____

   c) _____

2. Complete the sentences:

   a) Molars are best for _____

   b) Incisors are best for _____

   c) Canines are best for _____

Teeth

Tick the correct answers:

3. The hard outside of a tooth is called:
   a) enamel ☐
   b) dentine ☐
   c) roots ☐
   d) pulp ☐

4. Tooth decay is caused by:
   a) soft enamel ☐
   b) picking your teeth ☐
   c) bacteria that live in your stomach ☐
   d) bacteria that feed on sugar left in your mouth after eating ☐

5. Teeth contain:
   a) chlorine ☐
   b) chalk ☐
   c) calcium ☐
   d) cork ☐

6. Write four things you can do to look after your teeth:
   1. _____
   2. _____
   3. _____
   4. _____

TRY THIS

Activity

Baleen Whales, such as the Blue Whale, do not have teeth. They have up to 400 horny plates on each side of their upper jaw instead. The plates are covered in bristles and they work like sieves. Find out what Baleen Whales eat and how they sieve their food.

Check Your Progress!

Teeth ☐

Turn to page 48 and put a tick next to what you have just learned.

KS2: Living Things

Top Tip! Learning is fun, so if your child is tired, let them come back to this when they are fresh.

Parents Start Here...

In the curriculum the emphasis is on human nutrition rather than animal nutrition. Expand this topic with your child by looking at how people of different cultures eat different foods to us. You could buy or cook some foods that come from abroad.

Nutrition

Remember!

- Food is essential to provide energy for activity and growth.
- A varied diet is essential for good health.
- You can find out exactly what is in food by reading the labels.
- Carbohydrates give you energy.
- Proteins help you grow.
- Fats give you energy and help your brain to develop.
- Fibre helps your guts (bowels) to work properly.
- Vitamins and minerals help to keep your body in top shape.
- Water is essential to life.
- We all need five portions of fruit or vegetables a day.

1. The labels on four breakfast cereals show how much sugar each one contains. Which cereal is the best for your teeth? Circle the correct answer:

   a) 21 %   b) 48 %   c) 4 %   d) 33 %

2. Join the food type to the group of foods:

carbohydrates

fats

fibre

proteins

Nutrition

Tick the correct answers to these questions:

3. What percentage of your body is water?
   a) 70 % ✓
   b) 20 %
   c) 100%
   d) 10%

4. A healthy diet contains:
   a) no fats
   b) no sugar
   c) no fibre
   d) a variety of foods

5. Iron and calcium are important:
   a) proteins
   b) fats
   c) minerals
   d) carbohydrates

6. Describe your favourite meal and write about why it is good for you (or not!):

_____
_____
_____
_____

Activity

TRY THIS

Vegetarians do not eat meat or meat products. Meat contains the essential mineral **iron**. Find out what other foods vegetarians may eat to ensure they have enough iron in their diets. Girls and women need extra iron.

Check Your Progress!

Nutrition ☐

Turn to page 48 and put a tick next to what you have just learned.

KS2: Living Things

Top Tip! If your child struggles with anything, don't worry – let them go at their own pace.

Parents Start Here...

Ask your child to show you where their lungs and heart are. See if you can both locate other important organs.

Circulation: The Heart

Remember!

- The heart and lungs are important organs.
- The heart is a powerful muscle that pumps blood around the body.
- It pumps blood to the lungs where it picks up oxygen.
- Blood is carried around the body in blood vessels; through the arteries and veins.
- Arteries carry blood which is full of oxygen.
- Veins carry blood which has had the oxygen removed.
- Most arteries carry blood away from the heart.
- Most veins carry blood towards the heart.
- The heart and blood vessels are called the circulatory system.

1. Write in the missing words:

The heart and _____ _____ are called the circulatory system.

The heart is a large _____ that pumps blood around the body.

The heart pumps blood to the lungs where it picks up _____. It flows back to the heart, where it is _____ to all parts of the body through special vessels called _____. The oxygen is used up by the body.

The blood returns to the heart in special vessels called _____.

Once again, the _____ pumps the blood to the lungs.

Circle the correct answer:

2. The heart and lungs are both types of:

   a) limb   b) muscle   c) organ   d) intestine

Circulation: The Heart

Tick the correct answers:

3. Lungs take in oxygen and let out:
   a) oxygen
   b) air
   c) laughing gas
   d) carbon dioxide ✓

4. Lungs are found in the:
   a) chest ✓
   b) abdomen
   c) pelvis
   d) skull

5. The heart and blood vessels are known as the:
   a) central heating system
   b) reproductive system
   c) circulatory system
   d) arterial system

6. Arteries carry blood:
   a) to the heart
   b) through the lungs
   c) away from the heart
   d) in vessels called veins

Activity

Look at an adult's hand, wrist or legs and you may see some bulgy veins that are blue in colour. Blood that has had all of its oxygen removed is blue, not red. If your hands are warm, you may notice veins on your hands too.

Check Your Progress!
Circulation: The Heart
Turn to page 48 and put a tick next to what you have just learned.

KS2: Living Things

Parents Start Here...

Top Tip! Try and incorporate what your child learns into everyday life – they will remember it even better.

Observing and recording simple data is an essential part of scientific enquiry. Children need to learn how to plan experiments, and to obtain and present evidence.

Circulation: Exercise

Remember!

- When you exercise you need more *oxygen* to release the extra *energy* you are using.
- Exercise increases the *rate* at which your heart beats.
- You can *measure* your pulse to see how fast your heart is beating.
- You can *feel* your pulse in your neck or your wrist.

1. Match the pulse rate to the activity:

   a) 130 beats per minute   playing netball

   b) 105 beats per minute   writing in this book

   c) 65 beats per minute   sleeping

   d) 76 beats per minute   walking

Tick the correct answers:

2. When you exercise your pulse rate:
   a) goes up ☐   b) goes down ☐
   c) stays the same ☐ d) goes down then up ☐

3. When you rest after exercise your pulse rate:
   a) goes down ☐   b) goes up ☐
   c) goes up then down ☐ d) stays the same ☐

Circulation: Exercise

4. a) Measure your pulse rate for one minute and write the result here. This is your resting rate: 1 minute reading: _____ beats/minute

b) Run on the spot for one minute then record your pulse rate for a second time:
2 minute reading: _____ beats/minute

c) Record your pulse rate every minute until your pulse rate has returned to the first reading (a).
3 minute reading: _____ beats/minute
4 minute reading: _____ beats/minute
5 minute reading: _____ beats/minute
6 minute reading: _____ beats/minute

d) Make a graph of your results.

e) How long did it take your pulse rate to return to its resting rate?

f) When did your pulse rate decrease the most?

g) What do you think would happen to your pulse if you started doing exercise again?

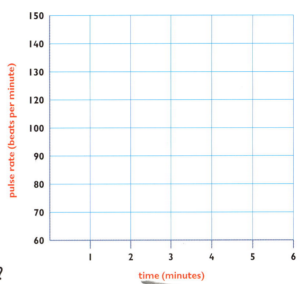

Activity

Repeat the pulse rate experiment, but this time use an adult volunteer. Do you think their pulse rate will start off higher or lower than yours? Do you think they will return to their resting rate as quickly as you?

Check Your Progress!
Circulation: Exercise
Turn to page 48 and put a tick next to what you have just learned.

KS2: Living Things

Top Tip! If your child loses concentration here, let them take a break.

Parents Start Here...

Show your child how biceps raise the upper arm by contracting. Help them locate their triceps on the underside of their upper arm and show them how contracting this lowers the arm.

Movement

Remember!

- Humans and some other animals have skeletons.
- Skeletons are made of bone.
- Bones are very strong but light.
- Bones protect delicate organs.
- Muscles are attached to bones.
- Muscles pull on the bones to make them move.

1. Complete the table. Use the diagram to help you.

SKULL – protects your brain, eyes and ears.

RIBS – protect your lungs and heart.

BACKBONE – contains and protects the nerves that carry messages from your brain to your body.

PELVIS – protects your digestive organs and helps you move your legs.

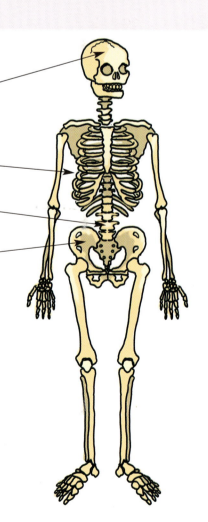

Name	What this bone protects
Skull	brain eyeballs
Rib cage	lungs heart
Backbone	nerves

16

Movement

Tick the correct answers:

2. When you lift your hand to your mouth, what happens to the muscle in your arm?
   a) It expands ☐   b) It twists ☐
   c) It contracts ☑   d) It pushes ☐

3. Which is the smallest bone?
   a) skull ☐   b) femur (thigh bone) ☐
   c) pelvis ☐   d) knee cap ☑

4. Which important mineral, found in dairy products, is needed for bones to grow and stay strong?
   a) iron ☐   b) copper ☐
   c) calcium ☑   d) nickel ☐

5. Where two bones connect is called a:
   a) limb ☐   b) organ ☐
   c) tissue ☐   d) joint ☑

6. The muscles in your upper arm are called:
   a) biceps and triceps ☑   b) bicycle and tricycle ☐
   c) femur and humerus ☐   d) tibia and fibula ☐

Activity

Animals that have skeletons inside their bodies are called vertebrates. Animals that do not have skeletons inside their bodies are called invertebrates. Can you think of three animals that are vertebrates? Can you think of three animals that are invertebrates? Is an octopus a vertebrate or an invertebrate?

Check Your Progress!

Movement ☐

Turn to page 48 and put a tick next to what you have just learned.

KS2: Living Things

Top Tip! Go through any of the questions on these pages as often as you like until your child understands it fully.

Parents Start Here...

By the end of Key Stage Two most children will have covered the topic of human reproduction, but they are only required to understand the principle stages of the human life cycle for their SATs.

Growth And Reproduction

Remember!

- Humans reproduce by having *babies*.
- Babies are completely *dependent* on their parents.
- Babies grow and *develop* into children.
- During *puberty* children mature into adults.
- As people get older their bodies *age* and change.
- Eventually everyone *dies*.

1. In the space on this page, draw the life cycle of a human, showing the key stages of birth, baby, child, puberty, adulthood, old age and death.

Growth And Reproduction

Tick the correct answers to these questions:

2. When animals, like butterflies, change completely during their life cycle we call it:
   a) larva ☐
   b) metamorphosis ☐
   c) camouflage ☐
   d) puberty ☐

3. Lizards begin life as:
   a) an egg ☑
   b) a larva ☐
   c) a worm ☐
   d) a chrysalis ☐

4. Look at these pictures of the life cycle of a frog. Label them with the numbers 1, 2 and 3, to show from youngest to oldest:

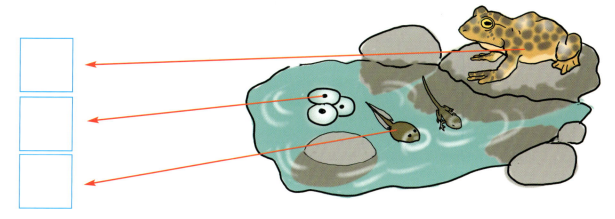

Activity

What do you think the world would be like if there was no death? Write a list of the advantages and disadvantages.

Check Your Progress! ☐
Growth And Reproduction
Turn to page 48 and put a tick next to what you have just learned.

KS2: Living Things

Top Tip! Always look for positive aspects to your child's work as well as helping them to resolve errors.

Parents Start Here...

Help your child understand that looking after their body now will provide rewards for the rest of their life. It is estimated, for example, that up to 60% of teenage girls are not getting enough calcium to prevent osteoporosis in later life, and that too many children are overweight due to lack of exercise.

Healthy Lives 1

Remember!

- To stay healthy, adults and children need to eat a *varied diet*.
- To stay healthy, adults and children need to drink plenty of *water* every day.
- *Exercise* is essential to keep our bodies working properly.

1. Why should people eat food that contains protein?

   _____
   _____
   _____

2. What are the other food groups everyone needs for a healthy diet?

   _____
   _____
   _____

3. Name two minerals necessary to keep a body healthy:

   _____
   _____

Healthy Lives 1

4. Which is the healthiest meal shown here? Tick the correct answer:

a)  ✓

c)  ☐

b) ☐

d)  ☐

Give reasons for your answer:

because it is good for you it gi'vs you enegie

5. Why is it a good idea for children to get some exercise every day?

So they dont get lazy and so g they get fit

6. List some activities that children might enjoy, while getting fit at the same time:

do how who ever dose the most h push ups wins

TRY THIS

Activity

Are you exercising every day? If not, ask your parents to help you find an enjoyable way to get out and get fit. There may be after-school activities or sports clubs you can join. Even walking to and from school is good exercise.

Check Your Progress!

Healthy Lives 1 ☐

Turn to page 48 and put a tick next to what you have just learned.

KS2: Living Things

Parents Start Here...

Top Tip! Learning is fun, so if your child is tired, let them come back to this when they are fresh.

Help your child with the task they have been set here. Beginning a dialogue about drugs, alcohol and smoking will make it easier for your child to come to you if they encounter these things outside the home.

Healthy Lives 2

Remember!

- Drugs may be addictive and may cause permanent damage to your body
- Smoking is bad for you. Cigarettes contain a drug, nicotine, which makes you addicted to them.
- Alcohol is a type of drug. It can become addictive. Large amounts of alcohol can damage your brain, liver, kidneys and other organs.
- Solvents, like glue and paint, are other types of drugs. Sniffing solvents can kill you instantly, or become addictive and cause damage to your brain.

1. Harry Jones is ten years old. He lives with his Mum and his older brother Nicky, who is 15. Nicky has got in with a gang of older boys, who like to drink beer, smoke cigarettes and even take drugs. Nicky has started to do all of these things too. Now Nicky does not eat his meals with the rest of the family and he has lost his place on the football team.

Harry is very worried about Nicky. Draw a leaflet that Harry could give to Nicky, explaining about healthy living and showing Nicky the damage he is doing to his body.

Healthy Lives 2

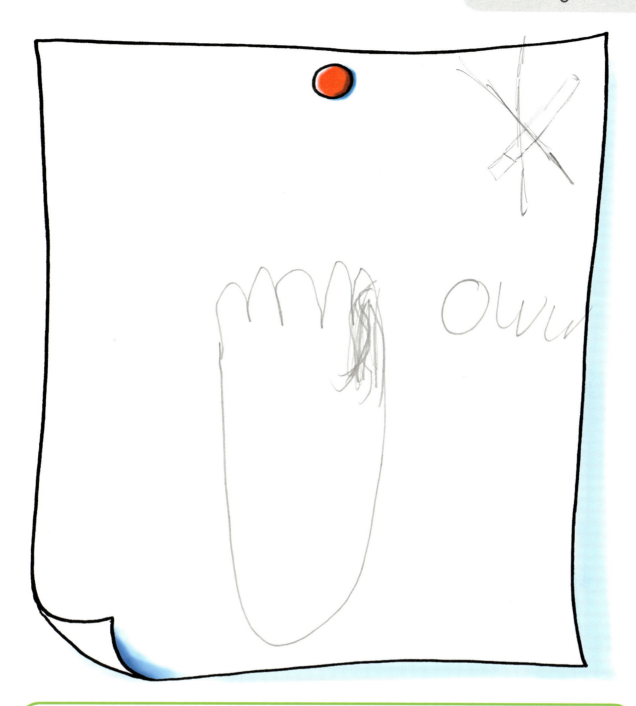

 ## Activity

Look in newspapers for stories about the bad effects that drugs and alcohol have had on people.

Check Your Progress!

Healthy Lives 2

Turn to page 48 and put a tick next to what you have just learned.

KS2: Living Things

Parents Start Here...

Ensure your child knows how to draw a simple plant and label it with the correct names and functions of its parts without reference to a book.

Top Tip! If your child struggles with anything, don't worry – let them go at their own pace.

The Structure Of Green Plants

Remember!

- Plants have roots and shoots.
- Roots anchor a plant into the soil and help the plant absorb water and minerals. Roots grow in the soil.
- Shoots grow towards the light. They may have stems, leaves and flowers.
- Flowers attract insects to a plant and the insects help a plant make seeds.
- Leaves are necessary for nutrition.
- Stems hold a plant up and move water and minerals from the roots to the leaves and flowers.

1. Tick the correct boxes in this table:

	flower	root	stem	leaf
a) The part of a plant involved in reproduction	✓			
b) The part of a plant involved in nutrition			✗	✓
c) The part of a plant that holds it up and moves towards the light	✗			
d) The part of a plant that absorbs water		✓		

The Structure Of Green Plants

2. Draw a picture of a simple green plant with a flower.
Label each part of the plant and describe what each part does.

Activity

A cactus is an unusual green plant that has adapted (changed) to suit life in dry countries. The stem is fat and stores water, while the leaves have become spines so that little water can evaporate from them. Find out how the leaves of the Venus Fly Trap have adapted.

KS2: Living Things

Parents Start Here...

Remind your child that although plants need minerals from the soil, these are not 'food'.

Green Plants: Growth And Nutrition 1

Remember!

- Green plants make their own food, using sunlight, water and carbon dioxide.
- This process is called photosynthesis.
- Photosynthesis occurs in leaves, using a green pigment (colour) called chlorophyll.
- Oxygen is a waste product of photosynthesis.
- Plants use the carbon dioxide that animals breathe out.

1. What are the three elements needed for plants to make their own food?

2. What is the name of this process?

3. Which gas is given off as a waste product of the process?

4. What is chlorophyll?

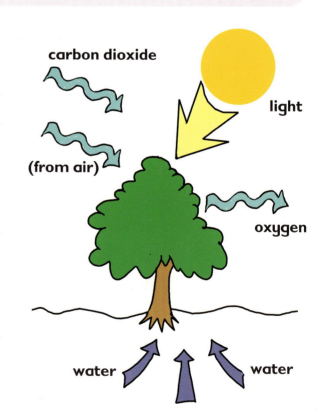

26

Green Plants: Growth And Nutrition 1

5. Animals have to move around to find food. Why don't plants have to move around?

because they Don't eat meat and There food gose to Them

6. Why do plants move their leaves towards the light?

go because they need light to grow

7. a) What would happen to a plant left in a dark place?

it ~~also~~ wold die.

b) Why?

because it needs ligh

8. a) What would happen to a plant that was never watered?

it wold die

b) Why?

because they need water to grow

Activity

TRY THIS

Lots of scientific words have been made up using Greek and Latin words. The word photo comes from the Greek word phos, which means 'light'. The word synthesis comes from the Greek word sunthesis which means 'to put together'.

Can you think of any other words that have the prefix 'photo–'?

Check Your Progress!
Green Plants: Growth And Nutrition 1
Turn to page 48 and put a tick next to what you have just learned.

KS2: Living Things

Top Tip! Try and incorporate what your child learns into everyday life – they will remember it even better.

Parents Start Here...

If your child has difficulty with the questions on these pages help them recreate the experiments so they can discover the answers for themselves.

Green Plants: Growth And Nutrition 2

Remember!

- You can carry out experiments to discover the effects of light, air, water and temperature on plant growth.
- You can carry out experiments to show what conditions a plant needs to grow.

Tick the correct answers to these questions:

1. Mark put some blue food colouring into a glass and added some water. He trimmed the stem of a white flower, then put the flower into the glass and left it in a warm room.

    After several days Mark noticed:
    a) The flower had died ☐
    b) The flower had turned blue ☑
    c) The stem had bent ☐

2. This experiment showed that:
    a) The water was blue ☐
    b) The flower was photosynthesising ☐
    c) Water travelled through the stem to the flower ☑

Green Plants: Growth And Nutrition 2

3. If Mark had used red food colouring instead, the flower would have:
   a) Turned red ✓
   b) Died ☐
   c) Turned into a fruit ☐

4. Liza put a twig with leaves into a glass of water. She poured a little cooking oil onto the water.

   After several days she noticed:
   a) The water level had stayed the same ☐
   b) The water level had gone down ☐
   c) The water level had gone up ☐

5. Liza realized that:
   a) The water was travelling up through the twig ✓
   b) The twig was dead ☐
   c) The twig was growing roots ☐

6. Liza had poured oil on the water:
   a) To stop bugs getting into it ☐
   b) So she could be sure that any change in the water level was due to the plant, not evaporation ☐
   c) To feed the twig ☐

Activity

TRY THIS

Have you done experiments like this at school? Talk about them with your Mum and Dad as this will help you to recall the things you learnt from the experiments.

Check Your Progress!
Green Plants: Growth And Nutrition 2 ☐
Turn to page 48 and put a tick next to what you have just learned.

KS2: Living Things

Top Tip! If your child loses concentration here, let them take a break.

Parents Start Here...

Buy a lily or similar large flower and help your child open it up to find all these plant parts.

The Parts Of A Flower

Remember!

- Flowers are used in reproduction.
- Their brightly coloured petals attract insects to them.
- The sepals are little leaves that protect the flower in bud.
- Flowers contain the male and female plant parts.
- The male plant part is called a stamen and contains an anther which is coated in pollen.
- The female plant parts is called a carpel and contains the stigma, the ovary (egg case) and ovules (eggs).
- The sticky stigma is the place that pollen lands, during pollination.
- The ovules develop into seeds.

1. Label the parts of the flower:

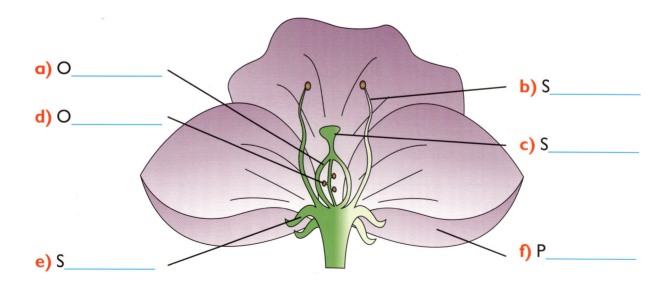

a) O_____
d) O_____
e) S_____
b) S_____
c) S_____
f) P_____

30

The Parts Of A Flower

2. Complete the sentences to describe each part of the flower:

a) The ovary is

_____

b) Stamens

_____

c) The stigma is

_____

d) Ovules are

_____

e) Sepals are

_____

f) Petals are

_____

Activity

You really need to know the names of all the parts of a flower and the jobs they do. Copy the picture onto a large piece of paper, with all the labels put in, and stick it somewhere you can see it every day.

Check Your Progress!
The Parts Of A Flower ☐
Turn to page 48 and put a tick next to what you have just learned.

KS2: Living Things

Parents Start Here...

Top Tip! If your child struggles with anything, don't worry – let them go at their own pace.

Children often get confused between fertilisation and pollination. Write the definitions on to pieces of paper and stick them somewhere your child will notice them every day.

Pollination And Fertilisation

Remember!

- When a grain of pollen is carried to a stigma we call it pollination.
- Wind or insects may be responsible for pollination.
- The grain of pollen contains a male sex cell.
- The male sex cell grows down to the ovary where it meets up with an ovule (egg).
- The male sex cell joins with the ovule. This is called fertilisation.
- A fertilised ovule can grow into a seed.

1. Tick the correct box for each statement:

Statement	True	False
A grain of pollen contains a male sex cell		
A male sex cell is carried to the stigma		
The male sex cell travels down to an ovule and fertilises it		
A fertilised egg grows into a seed		

2. Write a definition of pollination:

_____

_____

Pollination And Fertilisation

3. Write a definition of fertilisation:

   _____
   _____
   _____

4. Describe how pollen may get from one plant to another:

   _____
   _____
   _____

Tick the correct answers:

5. An ovule is:
   a) a male sex cell ☐
   b) a female sex cell (egg) ☐
   c) the site of pollination ☐
   d) a fruit ☐

6. The ovary contains:
   a) pollen ☐
   b) ovules ☐
   c) fruit ☐
   d) nectar ☐

Activity

Look closely at the petals of some flowers and you will see that they have faint lines which lead down to the centre of the flower. It is thought that these lines guide insects down to the sugary nectar which they like to eat. As the insects suck the nectar, they pollinate the flowers.

Check Your Progress!
Pollination And Fertilisation ☐
Turn to page 48 and put a tick next to what you have just learned.

KS2: Living Things

Top Tip! Always look for positive aspects to your child's work as well as helping them to resolve errors.

Parents Start Here...

Show your child how windborne seeds, like dandelion seeds, are light and can travel through the air.

Seeds And Fruits

Remember!

- Once fertilisation has taken place the ovary develops into a fruit.
- Some fruits are soft and juicy, like a strawberry.
- Some fruits are hard and tough, like a walnut.
- The fertilised ovule develops into a seed.
- Seeds are dispersed to the place where they may grow.
- Seeds may be dispersed by animals, the wind or when a seed pod dries and pops open.
- If conditions are right, a seed may be able to grow into a new plant (germination).
- Seeds need warmth, oxygen and water to germinate.

1. List three juicy fruits:

   _____
   _____
   _____

2. List two hard fruits:

   _____
   _____

3. Describe how a seed might be dispersed by wind:

   _____
   _____

Seeds And Fruits

4. Describe how a seed might be dispersed by an animal:

   _____

   _____

5. Describe how a seed might be dispersed by explosion:

   _____

   _____

6. Circle the three things a seed needs to grow:

   a) (sunlight)   d) (water)
   b) dark   e) birds
   c) (warmth)   f) oxygen

Tick the correct answer:

7. Germination is when:
   a) a pollen granule joins with an ovule ☐
   b) pollen reaches the stigma ☐
   c) a seed begins to grow ☐
   d) seeds are dispersed ☐

Activity

Ask an adult to help you germinate some seeds. Mustard, cress and beansprouts are all easy and quick to grow at home.

Check Your Progress!
Seeds And Fruits ☐
Turn to page 48 and put a tick next to what you have just learned.

KS2: Living Things

Top Tip! Remember to give your child lots of praise – they will work so much better.

Parents Start Here...

Help your child find out more about Charles Darwin. The Internet and library would be good places to start.

Living Things In Their Environments

Remember!

- **Environment** is the word used to describe the conditions that a plant or animal lives in.
- An animal's environment **controls** what types of food are available.
- Different environments might have different **climates** and weather conditions.
- Animals and plants have to be **suited** to their environment in order to survive.

Tick the correct answers:

1. This animal has adapted to the cold Antarctic environment by having a thick layer of fat to keep it warm. It also has a soft layer of downy feathers next to its skin to keep body heat in, and a layer of oily waterproof feathers to keep the cold water away.
    a) polar bear ✓
    b) herring
    c) penguin
    d) crocodile

2. This animal has adapted to the harsh conditions of the African desert. It can store water as fat in its body. Its feet are wide and can walk on sand without sinking in to it. This animal has very long eyelashes to keep sand out of its eyes.
    a) spitting cobra
    b) Jesus Christ lizard
    c) camel ✓
    d) parakeet

Living Things In Their Environments

3. Describe how a crocodile is suited to its life as a hunter in shallow waters.

4. Humans are very adaptable. Describe what you might do so you could live in a cold climate and in a hot climate:

a) Cold climate:

b) Hot climate:

Activity

Charles Darwin was a very great scientist of the Victorian age. He said that animals have to adapt to their environments in order to survive and breed. Find out some more about Charles Darwin. You will see his picture on the back of a ten pound note.

Check Your Progress!
Living Things In Their Environments
Turn to page 48 and put a tick next to what you have just learned.

KS2: Living Things

Top Tip! Go through any of the questions on these pages as often as you like until your child understands it fully.

Parents Start Here...

When children understand food chains and webs they are beginning to understand ecology and the whole concept of our dependence upon other living organisms.

Food Chains

Remember!

- Food chains show a relationship between plants and the animals that eat them.
- Nearly all food chains start with a green plant.
- Green plants make food. They are called primary producers.
- Animals that eat plants are called consumers.
- Predators are animals that hunt and eat other animals.
- Scavengers are animals that feed on animals that are already dead, often killed by another animal.
- Populations of animals can only increase if there is enough food to feed them.

1. Look at this food chain:

cabbage → snail → blackbird

a) Name the primary producer:

b) What animal does the blackbird eat?

c) Which animal is a predator?

38

Food Chains

2. A **habitat** is the place that an animal or plant lives. In which habitat might you find the food chain on page 38? Tick the correct answer:
   a) pond ☐
   b) garden ☐
   c) tropical rainforest ✓
   d) desert ☐

3. Look at this food chain:

   plankton → herring → lantern shark

   Plankton are tiny plants that drift near the surface of the oceans.

   a) Name the primary producer in this food chain:
   _____

   b) What part of the food chain is the herring?
   _____

   c) Imagine that many lantern sharks have been killed by fishermen. What would happen to the herring population?
   _____
   _____

4. Write a food chain that includes you as a predator:

   _____ → _____ → human

Activity

TRY THIS

Find out whether the famous dinosaur, Tyrannosaurus Rex, was a consumer of green plants, a predator or a scavenger.

Check Your Progress!
Food Chains ☐
Turn to page 48 and put a tick next to what you have just learned.

KS2: Living Things

Parents Start Here...

Top Tip! Try and incorporate what your child learns into everyday life – they will remember it even better.

The curriculum requires that children understand that micro-organisms may be either beneficial or harmful.

Micro-Organisms

Remember!

- **Micro-organisms** are tiny living creatures that are too small to be seen with the naked eye.
- Micro-organisms can be studied using **microscopes**.
- Micro-organisms are neither plants nor animals; they are put in a **separate group** of their own.
- Some micro-organisms are useful, e.g. **yeast**.
- Some micro-organisms are dangerous, e.g. **viruses**.
- **Viruses**, **bacteria** and some **fungi** are types of micro-organism.

1. Viruses are micro-organisms that often cause disease and colds. List three things you can do to prevent the spread of colds and diseases:

_____

_____

_____

2. Bacteria break down, or rot, dead things and food. Fill in the missing words:

a) There are bacteria in your stomach. They help to b_____k down the f_____d.

b) Bacteria can cause food-p_____g in the kitchen.

c) Bacteria help to break down dead plants and turn them back into s_____l.

d) Some bacteria are used to make food such as ch_____e and yo_____t.

40

Micro-Organisms

3. Yeast is a very useful fungus. Circle the two things that yeast helps to make:

4. Write down some simple steps you could take in the kitchen to prevent food-poisoning:

_____
_____
_____
_____

5. What piece of equipment would you use to study micro-organisms?
Tick the correct answer:
   a) telescope
   b) microscope
   c) binoculars
   d) periscope ✓

Activity

Put a piece of bread in a saucer and pour a little water over the top. Leave it somewhere warm and you will be able to watch black pin-mould grow over the bread's surface. Keep it away from other food and do not touch the bread. Get an adult's permission before you do this experiment!

Check Your Progress!
Micro-Organisms
Turn to page 48 and put a tick next to what you have just learned.

41

KS2: Living Things

Parents Start Here...

Top Tip! Learning is fun, so if your child is tired, let them come back to this when they are fresh.

Children are required to think about sorting objects according to similar characteristics in maths too. They need to analyse the information they have, then weigh up the importance of different characteristics.

Classifying Animals And Plants

Remember!

- Animals and plants have been sorted into groups.
- This sorting is called classification.
- Animals and plants are grouped according to their similar characteristics.
- Classifying living organisms helps us to name them.
- Classifying living organisms can help us understand how they are related to one another.

1. Write the names of 5 plants that grow flowers:

   _____
   _____
   _____
   _____
   _____

2. Write the names of 3 animals that can swim:

   _____
   _____
   _____

Classifying Animals And Plants

3. What are animals that have backbones called? Circle the correct answer:

   vertebrates   invertebrates

4. Name three vertebrate animals and three invertebrate animals:

   vertebrates: invertebrates:

   _____   _____

   _____   _____

   _____   _____

5. Look at the animal characteristics in this table. Tick the type of vertebrate that has each characteristic and write the name of an example in the box.

characteristic \ animal	Mammal e.g. human	Fish e.g. trout	Amphibian e.g. frog	Bird e.g. sparrow	Reptile e.g. snake
a) Has feathers and lays eggs					
b) Has fur and gives birth					
c) Has a wet skin and breathes through gills when young					
d) Lays eggs on dry land and has a scaly skin					
e) Breathes in water using gills					

Activity

Animals and plants are often given Latin names when they are classified. This makes it easier for scientists all over the world to know they are talking about the same organism. Find out the Latin name for humans.

Check Your Progress!
Classifying Animals And Plants
Turn to page 48 and put a tick next to what you have just learned.

KS2: Living Things

Top Tip! Remember to give your child lots of praise – they will work so much better.

Parents Start Here...

Children are expected to know how to make and use a simple key. They need to understand that the variety of plants and animals makes it important to identify and assign them to groups.

Keys

Remember!

- **Keys** are used to identify *plants* and *animals*.
- Using a key helps us decide which group a particular animal or plant belongs to.
- A key is a series of questions. They are usually 'yes' or 'no' questions.

1. Work through this key to identify a mystery animal:

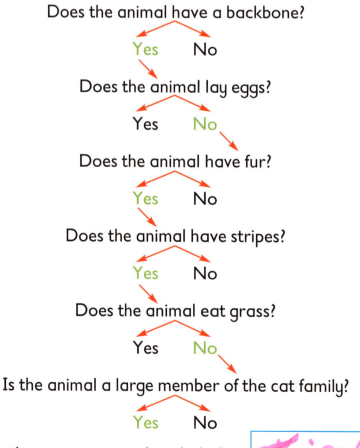

Does the animal have a backbone? Yes → No
Does the animal lay eggs? Yes → No
Does the animal have fur? Yes → No
Does the animal have stripes? Yes → No
Does the animal eat grass? Yes → No
Is the animal a large member of the cat family? Yes → No

What do you think the mystery animal might be?

Tiger

2. Use this space to write your own key to help identify any animal or plant you choose:

Keys

Activity

Play twenty questions with friends or family. You have to think of an animal and everyone else has to ask you questions about it. You are only allowed to answer 'yes' or 'no' and only twenty questions are allowed before they have to guess the animal.

Check Your Progress!

Keys

Turn to page 48 and put a tick next to what you have just learned.

KS2: Living Things

Answers

Pages 4–5
1. b
2. d
3. d
4. c
5. a
6. b
7. b
8. Movement, nutrition, sensitivity, reproduction, excretion, respiration and growth

Pages 6–7
1. b
2. c
3. a
4. c
5. b
6. b

Pages 8–9
1. a) molar
b) canine
c) incisor
2. a) Molars are best for grinding and chewing food.
b) Incisors are best for cutting and chopping food.
c) Canines are best for tearing food.
3. a
4. d
5. c
6. Brush your teeth with fluoride, visit the dentist, floss your teeth, eat non-sugary foods, drink water and milk, avoid fizzy drinks.

Pages 10–11
1. c
2. meat, milk, butter, oil = fats
milk, meat, fish, eggs = proteins
bread, pasta, potatoes, rice = carbohydrates
pasta, rice, cereal, fruit = fibre
3. a
4. d
5. c

Pages 12–13
1. The heart and blood vessels are called the circulatory system. The heart is a large organ (or muscle) that pumps blood around the body. The heart pumps blood to the lungs where it picks up oxygen. It flows back to the heart, where it is carried to all parts of the body through special vessels called arteries. The oxygen is used up by the body. The blood returns to the heart in special vessels called veins. Once again, the heart pumps the blood to the lungs.
2. c
3. d
4. a
5. c
6. c

Pages 14–15
1. a = playing netball
b = walking
c = sleeping
d = writing in this book
2. a
3. a

Pages 16–17
1. The skull protects the brain, eyes and ears, the rib cage protects the heart and lungs and the backbone protects the spinal cord (nerves).
2. c
3. d
4. c
5. d
6. a

Pages 18–19
2. b
3. a
4.

3
1
2

Pages 20–21
1. Protein helps the body replace dead cells, repair itself and grow.
2. Fats, carbohydrates and fibre.
3. Calcium and iron
4. (a) is the best meal because it is varied; it has protein, carbohydrates and fat and fibre as well as calcium in the milk.
5. Exercise keeps your body fit and working properly. It helps develop your skeleton and muscles. It also helps your brain learn co-ordination and other skills.

Pages 24–25
1. a = flower
b = leaf
c = stem
d = root

2.
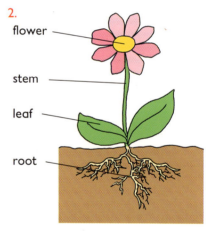

flower
stem
leaf
root

(see Remember! box for functions)

Pages 26–27
1. Sunlight, water and carbon dioxide
2. Photosynthesis
3. Oxygen
4. A green pigment, necessary for photosynthesis.
5. The things plants need to make food are all around them.
6. Photosynthesis takes place in leaves, so they need to face the light.
7. It would eventually die because it can not make food without light.
8. It would wilt and then die because it can not make food without water.

Answers

Pages 28–29
1. b
2. c
3. a
4. b
5. a
6. b

Pages 30–31
1.

2. a) The *ovary* is the place where the eggs (ovules) grow.
b) *Stamens* carry pollen which contains the male sex cell.
c) The *stigma* is a female part of the flower.
d) *Ovules* are eggs and contain the female sex cell.
e) *Sepals* are little leaves that protect the budding flower.
f) *Petals* are brightly coloured and lead an insect into the flower.

Pages 32–33
1. They are all true.
2. Pollination occurs when a grain of pollen is carried to a stigma.
3. Fertilisation is the joining of a male sex cell with an ovule.
4. Pollen may get from one plant to another by wind carrying it, on an animal's fur or on the back of an insect.
5. b
6. b

Pages 34–35
1. Strawberry, cherry, peach, etc.
2. Walnut, peanut, brazil nut, etc.
3. Lightweight seeds may be carried by the wind. They are often small or have a special shape that helps them stay airborne.
4. Seeds may get caught in an animal's fur – some even have little hooks to help this process. Or a seed may be eaten by an animal and pass through its body.
5. Some seed pods can explode when they have dried out at the end of the summer. The seeds inside get propelled away from the plant.
6. Seeds need warmth, water and oxygen to grow.
7. c

Pages 36–37
1. c
2. c
3. A crocodile has a long and slender body that is difficult to see in water. Its colour matches the murky shallows. Its teeth are sharp and its jaws are strong. A crocodile's eyes can poke above the water to watch for food while the rest of its body is hidden.

Pages 38–39
1. a) cabbage
b) snail
c) blackbird
2. b
3. a) plankton
b) consumer
c) Without any predators, the herring population would explode (get larger). Some herring might starve because there would not be enough plankton to feed them all.
4. Example: grass ➡ cow ➡ human

Pages 40–41
1. When people are ill they should stay away from other people, use a handkerchief to catch coughs and sneezes and wash their hands regularly so they do not pass the virus on.
2. a) There are bacteria in your stomach. They help to *break* down the *food*.
b) Bacteria can cause *food-poisoning* in the kitchen.
c) Bacteria help to break down dead plants and turn them back into *soil*.
d) Some bacteria are used to make food such as *cheese* and *yogurt*.
3. Beer and bread
4. Throw away out of date food, store cooked and uncooked food separately in a fridge, keep food covered at all times, cook it thoroughly, clean the work surfaces and dry them, wash your hands.
5. b

Pages 42–43
3. vertebrates
4. Look at Question 5 to get some help with this question! Invertebrates are the animals that do not fit into any of these categories. (Think of some mini-beasts.)
5. a = bird
b = mammal
c = amphibian
d = reptile
e = fish

Pages 44–45
1. A tiger

47

Check Your Progress!

Check Your Progress!

Life Processes: Humans And Animals .... ☐

Life Processes: Plants .... ☐

Teeth .... ☐

Nutrition .... ☐

Circulation: The Heart .... ☐

Circulation: Exercise .... ☐

Movement .... ☐

Growth And Reproduction .... ☐

Healthy Lives 1 .... ☐

Healthy Lives 2 .... ☐

The Structure Of Green Plants .... ☐

Green Plants: Growth And Nutrition 1 .... ☐

Green Plants: Growth And Nutrition 2 .... ☐

The Parts Of A Flower .... ☐

Pollination And Fertilisation .... ☐

Seeds And Fruits .... ☐

Living Things In Their Environments .... ☐

Food Chains .... ☐

Micro-Organisms .... ☐

Classifying Animals And Plants .... ☐

Keys .... ☐